The front cover

Read the title. What is the setting of this story?

How would you feel if you knew a monster was coming to your village?

What might be the first sign that it had arrived? (*shouting, roaring,* etc.)

The Monster is Coming!

It's just another boring day at school for Simon, except for the large hairy monster stamping down the street outside. Can Simon save the day?

OBJECTIVE
To re-tell story through role play

GOLD LEVEL

ISBN 0-433-02898-3
9 780433 028963

The back cover

Let's read the blurb together.

What would you do if a monster came stamping past the school?

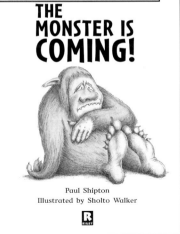

THE
MONSTER IS
COMING!

Paul Shipton
Illustrated by Sholto Walker

The title page

Is this a fierce monster? Why do you think that?

How does the monster look as though he is feeling?

What might be the problem?

Lesson 1 (Chapter 1)

READ

Read pages 2 to 5

Purpose: To find out why the villagers were frightened and what they thought might happen.

PAUSE

Pause at page 5

Find a word on page 2 that tells us what Simon is like. (*dreamily*)

Why were the people frightened? How do we know? (*they were shouting*)

What did some people think the monster might do? (*eat them, crush them*)

What was the first thing they heard that told them the monster had arrived? (*booming sound of giant footsteps*)

How tall was the monster? (*as tall as a tree*)

What happened to Simon? (*He lost his teacher.*)

Chapter 1

It was a Monday morning. The village children were all at school. Simon was looking dreamily out of the window.

Suddenly Simon heard a shout. "Run! Hide!" someone cried.

The children looked out of the window. People were running away. Some people were shouting. They all looked afraid.

A woman ran into the school.

"Run!" she shouted. "Hide! There's a monster in the village! It'll eat us! It'll crush us in our homes!"

"Don't be silly!" said the teacher.

Then they heard the booming sound of giant footsteps. A huge monster, as tall as a tree, stamped past their school. It shook its giant, hairy head from side to side and roared loudly.

"We should hide in the village hall," said the teacher sensibly. "Line up in the school playground."

The playground was full of people. Somehow, Simon lost the teacher.

2

3

4

5

READ

Read pages 6 to 8

Purpose: To find out what happens to Simon, and find out how the villagers feel about the monster.

PAUSE

Pause at page 8

How did Simon feel? (*afraid but curious*)

How are the villagers feeling? Find the words on page 8 (*half afraid, half angry, shook their fists, picture of angry faces*). What do they decide to do?

Read aloud what they say they are going to do. How would they say it?

Simon was afraid, but he wanted to see what was going on. It's not often you see a monster in your village! The monster was going towards the village square. Simon followed it.

There were lots of villagers in the village square. The monster was sitting in the middle of the square. It was still roaring loudly.

6

7

The villagers were half afraid, but half angry too.

"Who does this monster think it is?" asked one man angrily. The villagers shook their fists.

"We should chase it away!" shouted a woman. They picked up a long log.

"One, two, three . . . charge!"

8

The villagers charged. The monster gave an even louder roar. The roar was so loud it blew them over.

9

READ

Read pages 9 to 12

Purpose: To find out what happens when the villagers try to chase the monster away.

PAUSE

Pause at page 12

What happened when the villagers tried to chase the monster away? (*He roared and blew them over.*)

Why does the baker give bread and cakes to the monster? (*He thought the monster might be hungry.*) Does the monster eat them?

How does the baker feel? (*insulted and angry*)

What do the villagers do next? (*make a fire to warm the monster*) How does the monster feel?

Please turn to page 15 for Revisit and Respond activities.

"It might want something to eat," said
the village baker.
He filled a tub with bread and cakes.
A few villagers took the tub to the monster.
Then they ran away quickly.

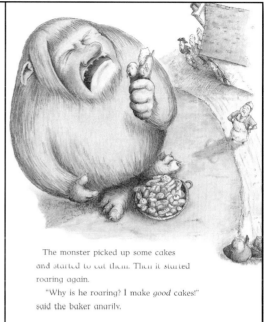

The monster picked up some cakes
and started to eat them. Then it started
roaring again.
"Why is he roaring? I make *good* cakes!"
said the baker angrily.

"The monster might be too cold," said an
old man. So the villagers made a fire.
"It will be warm now," said the old man.

Lesson 2 (Chapter 2)

RECAP

Recap lesson 1

What has happened in the village?

How do the villagers feel about the monster?

What have they tried to do with the monster? Has anything worked?

What's the name of the boy in the story?

READ

Read pages 13 to 16

Purpose: To find out what Simon discovers about the monster.

Chapter 2

The monster roared again. The roar was so loud it blew the fire out.

"What now?" asked the villagers.

Nobody knew what to do. Then Simon had an idea. He picked up a stick and ran into the square.

13

"Come back!" a man shouted.

"Stop him!" shouted an old woman.

It was too late. Simon ran towards the monster. Simon used the stick to draw a picture on the dusty ground. It was a picture of a boy. The monster just looked at him.

First Simon pointed to the boy. Then he pointed to himself. He said his name loudly, "Simon."

The monster nodded. It understood.

14

15

PAUSE

Pause at page 16

What do the villagers do when they see Simon getting closer to the monster? (*try to stop him*)

Read what the villagers say. How do you think they say it? (*exclamation marks*)

What does Simon find out about the monster? (*his name*) How does he do it?

What do you think might happen next?

READ

Read pages 17 to 19

Purpose: To find out what Simon's plan is to help the monster.

PAUSE

Pause at page 19

What is the monster's problem?

What is Simon's plan?

How do we know how loudly the monster is roaring? (*hats blew off the villagers, leaves blew off the trees, curtains blew out of the houses*)

Do you think Simon's plan will work?

Next, Simon drew a much bigger picture on the ground. It was a picture of the monster. Simon pointed to the picture, and then to the monster. At last the monster spoke.

"BLOG," said the monster. Simon smiled and nodded, because he understood. Its name was Blog!

Suddenly, the monster picked up a big log. It drew a picture of a monster, but this one was even bigger. It was huge. The monster pointed at this picture sadly. Then it began to roar even louder.

All at once, Simon understood. The monster was roaring because it wanted someone!

"Of course!" he shouted to the villagers. "It's not angry – it's lost!"

"But what should we do?" asked one villager.

"We should get it to roar even louder," said Simon. "Then another monster might hear it."

"How can we do that?" asked another villager.

Simon stood close to the monster. Then Simon roared and roared as loudly as he could. The monster looked puzzled.

Then it began to roar. It roared so loudly that the hats blew off the villagers.

Then it roared even more loudly so the leaves blew off the trees!

Then it roared more loudly still, so the curtains blew out of the houses.

READ

Read pages 20 to 23

Purpose: To find out if Simon's plan worked.

PAUSE

Pause at page 23

Turn to page 20. What are the first signs that the giant monster was coming? (*booming footsteps, ground shaking, the square went dark*)

Which words tell you that the giant monster was gentle? (*careful not to crush any houses*)

How do you know the baby monster was pleased? (*laughed*)

How did the giant monster show it was happy? (*It drew a smile.*)

Suddenly, there was a boom in the distance. The ground shook. Then there was another louder boom.

Something was coming, and it was big. Suddenly, the square was dark. Something was blocking the sunlight.

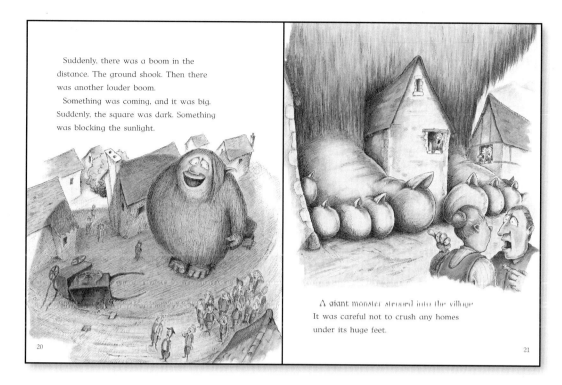

A giant monster stepped into the village. It was careful not to crush any homes under its huge feet.

The smaller monster looked up and started to laugh. The giant monster picked up the smaller monster with one huge hand.

Then the giant monster bent down and started to draw. It drew a smile on the picture of the big monster.

Simon understood. The monster had found its child. He looked up at the little monster and smiled.

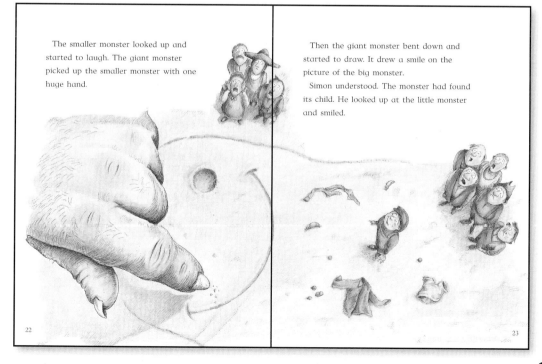

20

21

22

23

13

Then the two monsters stamped off towards the mountains.

24

READ

Read to the end

Purpose: To find out what the monsters do.

PAUSE

Pause at page 24

How do you think Simon feels when the two monsters stamp away?

After Reading

Revisit and Respond

Lesson 1

T How do the villagers know the monster is unhappy? (*roaring*)

T How do the villagers change their attitude towards the monster? (*tried to chase him, then tried to help him*)

T What have they done so far to try to make him feel better? (*given him cakes, lit a fire*) Will this work?

T What would you do to help the monster feel better? What do you think the problem is?

S Read page 4 aloud with expression. The children could perhaps take it in turns to be the woman/the teacher.

Lesson 2

T Ask the children which words on page 22 tell us how big the giant monster was. (*She picked up the small monster with one huge hand.*)

T Discuss the characters of Simon and the little monster. Think of adjectives to describe them.

T Role-play a TV interview with the baker and Simon, to describe the events of the day. First, the children could brainstorm questions an interviewer might ask.

S On page 19, find the words which tell us the monster was roaring louder and louder. (*so loudly, even more loudly, more loudly still*)

Follow-up

Independent Group Activity Work

This book is accompanied by two photocopy masters, one with a reading focus, and one with a writing focus, which support the main teaching objectives of this book. The photocopy masters can be found in the Planning and Assessment Guide.

PCM 45 (*reading*)

PCM 46 (*writing*)

Writing

Guided writing: Look at pages 6 and 7. Create a freeze-frame where children take the roles of villagers. Ask them questions about how they are feeling and write their answers down.

Extended writing: Imagine a monster passes by your school one day. Describe what happens.

Assessment Points

Assess that the children have learnt the main teaching points of the book by checking that they can:

- retell the story using dialogue and narrative from the text
- identify and describe characters, expressing own views and using words and phrases from the text
- read aloud with intonation and expression appropriate to the grammar and punctuation.